The Jelly That Wouldn't Wobble

D1354298

'The Jelly That Wouldn't Wobble'

An original concept by Angela Mitchell

© Angela Mitchell

Illustrated by Sarah Horne

Published by MAVERICK ARTS PUBLISHING LTD

Studio 3A, City Business Centre, 6 Brighton Road,

Horsham, West Sussex, RH13 5BB

© Maverick Arts Publishing Limited June 2016

+44 (0)1403 256941

ISBN 978-1-84886-225-8

www.maverickbooks.co.uk

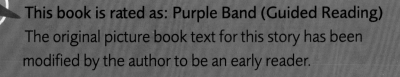

This book is rated as: Purple Band (Guided Reading)
The original picture book text for this story has been
modified by the author to be an early reader.

The **Jelly** That Wouldn't **Wobble**

By **Angela Mitchell**

Illustrated by **Sarah Horne**

Princess Lolly wriggled and jiggled on her throne.

It was her 89th birthday party.

"Where's my special jelly?" she asked.

"Here, Your Highness!" replied the guard.

The cook and his assistant proudly carried in

the special jelly.

Everyone gasped.

The jelly was GLORIOUS!

Princess Lolly squealed with excitement.

She prodded the jelly... and then looked puzzled.

"This jelly doesn't wobble!" cried

Princess Lolly in horror.

The cook prodded the jelly too.

"Doesn't wobble? Doesn't wobble?"

said the cook, in a fluster. "Of course it

wobbles, Your Highness: it's jelly!"

"I. SAY. THIS. JELLY. DOESN'T. WOBBLE!"

screeched the Princess. She prodded the jelly

again and again... and again. It didn't wobble!

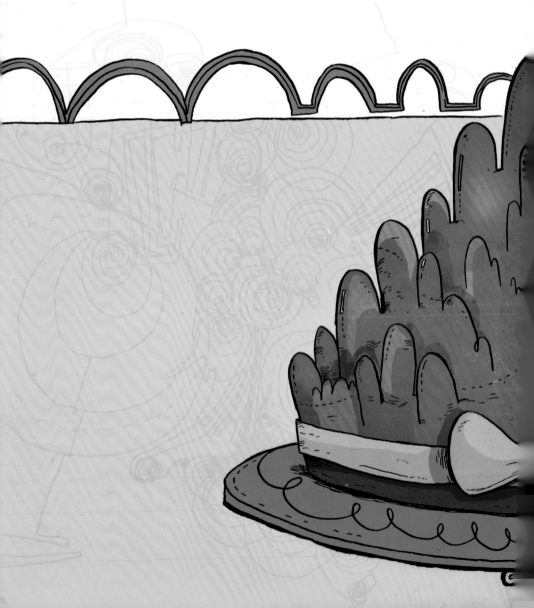

"I want my jelly to wobble! WHY. WON'T. MY. JELLY. WOBBLE?" she yelled. A royal tear rolled down her cheek.

Everyone looked at the jelly in wonder.

"I don't WANT to be eaten!" growled the jelly.

Princess Lolly slumped on her throne.

"MELT THAT JELLY!" boomed the Princess.

"Your Highness, NO!" begged the cook.

"Think of the mess, Your Highness," said the guard.

Princess Lolly thought for a moment.

"I will give a thousand and one chocolate coins to anyone who can make this jelly wobble!" announced the Princess.

Everyone gasped...

"I'll prod it with my walking stick!" said

the oldest guest. That didn't work.

"Rock the table!" shouted the twin guests.

That didn't work.

"Scare it!" the royal window cleaner hollered.

He pulled some horrible faces. That didn't work.

The jelly still refused to wobble.

"I WON'T WOBBLE AND THAT'S THAT!"

screamed the jelly.

Princess Lolly turned red with anger.

The cook turned white with worry.

"I know how to make it wobble,"

said the smallest guest.

"You do?" boomed the Princess.

"Yes, Your Highness," said the smallest guest proudly.

"Make the jelly really, really, really cold.

Then it will shiver and wobble!"

"Wonderful!" said the cook, excited.

"Go on, then!" Princess Lolly ordered.

"We need ice cream," whispered

the smallest guest to the cook.

"Of course!" gasped the cook.

The guard fetched a wobbly old ladder and the

royal ice cream scoop. The cook placed three

scoops of tutti frutti ice cream on top of the jelly.

Everyone held their breath. The jelly tried

very hard not to shiver...

The ice cream began to melt

and trickle down the jelly's sides.

"I saw something move!" gasped the smallest guest.

"Oh, please wobble," begged the cook.

"B*rrrrrr*!" The jelly suddenly shivered.

"B*rrrrrrrrrrrrrrrrrrr*!"

It shivered again, rocking this way and that. Soon it was quivering and quaking, trembling and shaking.

What a spectacle!

The guests moved back in fear, and the cook

began to cry. Princess Lolly stared in wonder at

the jelly, as it...

WOBBLED and WIBBLED, WIBBLED and

WOBBLED, just as a royal jelly should!

The hungry guests cheered, and so did the cook.

"SILENCE!" cried Princess Lolly. There was an

instant hush.

"Now we can eat jelly!" the Princess cried.

"Phew," sighed the cook.

And they did.

Quiz

1. How old is Princess Lolly?

a) 9

b) 99

c) 89

2. What is the reward for making the jelly wobble?

a) A thousand and one chocolate coins

b) A thousand pounds

c) A million golden coins

3. What does the oldest guest do to try and make the jelly wobble?

a) Shake it

b) Shout at it

c) Poke it with a walking stick

4. Princess Lolly turned _____ with anger.

a) Pink

b) Orange

c) Red

5. What flavour is the ice cream?

a) Tutti Frutti

b) Raspberry

c) Chocolate

Turn over for answers

Light Pink

Dark Pink

Red (End of Yr R)

Yellow

Blue

Green

Orange

Turquoise (End of Yr 1)

Purple

Gold

White (End of Yr 2)

Lime

Book Bands for Guided Reading

The Institute of Education book banding system is made up of twelve colours, which reflect the level of reading difficulty. The bands are assigned by taking into account the content, the language style, the layout and phonics.

Children learn at different speeds but the colour chart shows the levels of progression with the national expectation shown in brackets. To learn more visit the IoE website: www.ioe.ac.uk.

Maverick early readers have been adapted from the original picture books so that children can make the essential transition from listener to reader. All of these books have been book banded for guided reading to the industry standard and edited by a leading educational consultant.

Quiz Answers: 1c, 2a, 3c, 4c, 5a